A Daughter of the Holocaust

Melanie Sol

A Daughter of the Holocaust

Copyright © 2024

All rights reserved.

ISBN:9798320246079

A Daughter of the Holocaust

I dedicate this work to my grandparents, my aunt and my uncle. The ones whose hopes and dreams were extinguished in Auschwitz. May their memories be a blessing.

A Daughter of the Holocaust

A Daughter of the Holocaust

Melanie Sol

A Daughter of the Holocaust

I was born on December 7, 1956 and yet, as the title of this account describes, I am "a daughter of the Holocaust." You ask, "How can that be given the Holocaust took place between the years of 1939 and 1945?" To my own shock and amazement, having been raised by my dad who is a Holocaust survivor, I feel as though I have lived through the Holocaust myself. The same emotional and psychological effects that my dad has taken away from his time in the concentration camp have become part of my personality. I see the same effects manifesting in the personalities of my siblings.

I often wondered why a dark cloud always hung above my head. A spirit of doom and gloom hovered around me. My siblings and I had taken on an identity of being constantly miserable. We had learned that the world is a horrible and scary place. Unintentionally, my dad instilled fear in us. He was very overprotective. If we were out and did not call him, he became distraught with worry, imagining something terrible had happened to us. After all these years, at age 51, I have learned the name of what my siblings and I experienced living with my dad. It is called, "Secondary Post Traumatic Stress Syndrome."

NIGHTMARES

In my home, as a young child, I remember hearing my dad wailing in his sleep as he had nightmares about the Holocaust. Before his passing I asked him what some of those nightmares were about. He would dream about how emaciated he was, about the striped jacket and pants he had to wear. He would try in his dream to get out of this "gehenom" (Yiddish for the word "hell"). He would picture the bunks he had to sleep in. A bunk consisted of three shelves of flat boards and although each shelf was only big enough for two or three men, they had to squeeze 6 or 7 men on each shelf of the bunk. The men were of all different sizes. Some men carried disease or would vomit or have diarrhea as they lay very tightly next to you. "It was torture," my dad said, and he would ask himself, "Why do I deserve this life? Only because I was born a Jew? What did I do? Why me?" My mom would have to wake him up to stop the horrible nightmare from continuing.

My mom died when I was thirteen years old. My dad's dreams continued, and when I heard him wailing again in his sleep, to help stop the nightmare I would yell to him from my bedroom to wake up. The wails were heart wrenching. As young children, it was beyond our comprehension to grasp the horrors my dad and his family had faced. As we grew up through the teenage years my dad did not speak to us about the horrors of the Holocaust. What he did share with us was what his life was like before Hitler invaded Poland, before his life was changed forever.

Melanie's parents, Murray and Jean Hauptman Sol

CHILDHOOD IN POLAND

My father was born on April 12, 1922 in Plonsk, Poland. He was the third of four children. The eldest was his brother Aaron, his sister, Miriam, who they called Mannia, my dad, Moishe and, finally, his brother Solomon. His dad's name was Israel Sol and his mom's name was Nicha Sol. Nicha's maiden name was Lazenski.

"Bubba" and Nicha Lazenski Sol

A Daughter of the Holocaust

My dad's family followed Orthodox Judaism. My paternal grandfather, Israel, was a tailor and my grandmother, Nicha, a seamstress. My grandmother Nicha Lazenski Sol had twelve siblings. The small town of Plonsk in Poland where they lived consisted mostly of my father's aunts, uncles and cousins. Needless to say it was a huge family. My great-grandmother Lazenski lived to the ripe old age of 103 in that little town after giving birth to 13 children. My dad refers to her as "my Bubba" (Yiddish for grandmother). In her younger days she had a fruit store in the town and sold fruit for living.

Nicha and "Bubba" with two cousins. The young boy standing in front is Murray's eldest brother Aaron, who, after making Aliyah to Israel before the start of WWII, adopted the name Melach.

He remembered visiting her home every day as a young child with his mother. They loved spending time together. He would run errands for his grandmother. She would give him goodies and some coins to spend. My dad said when the Germans entered Poland, they took his grandmother to the hospital and he never saw her again. He only had a picture of her to remember her by. His mother Nicha's oldest sister, who came to the United States way before the war, saved the picture. Nicha hardly knew this sister because she was the youngest of 13 children and there was a big age difference between the oldest and the youngest child. As my dad would gaze at the picture of his grandmother Lazenski, it brought back many fond memories.

From birth to the age of seventeen my father had a wonderful childhood. He was very close to his parents, especially his mother, to his siblings and all his relatives. They would have memorable picnics together and enjoy frequent visits to each other's homes. My dad would speak of all the Jewish Holidays when the family would get together. He spoke of the great meals his mother and grandmother prepared. In those days there was no such thing as a refrigerator. All the food was kept cool in the basement of the house in cooler boxes. As a result, all the food was bought and prepared fresh almost daily. There was no such thing as chemical additives to extend the shelf life of the food they ate. When my dad came to America and had refrigeration, he always liked to go to the supermarket, meat store and produce store every few days to buy fresh food. He did not like to keep food too long in the refrigerator or freezer and ate very little food containing preservatives. Even at eighty-six years old my father was very disciplined in his eating habits. This was instilled in him as a child growing up in Poland.

In spite of the great family life my dad experienced as a child, outside the home was a totally different story. There was a great deal of Anti-Semitism by the Polish Catholics in his town. The Catholic children went to school in the morning and the Jewish children went to school in the afternoon. They were not allowed to go to school together or mingle. When they passed each other going to and from school, the Polish children would call the Jewish children "Christ Killers." They would then proceed to beat up the Jewish children. My father tells the story of one particular boy who beat him up every day. He would run home to his mother crying every day. She would say," if you stand up to him once and fight back he will never bother you again". So that's what my father did and it worked! That young boy never did bother my father again. I think this was one lesson my father learned that was instrumental in helping him to survive concentration camp.

(Below) Here are pictures of Murray (Moishe) Sol after liberation and before he passed away in 2011

His mother Nicha Lazenski Sol and his sister Miriam.

THE GHETTO

My dad was 17 years old when Hitler invaded Poland in September of 1939. His parents were both 40 years old. His sister, Miriam, was 20 years old and his younger brother, Solomon, was 16 years old. His older brother, Aaron, left Poland a few years before the invasion to go to Palestine to help establish a Zionistic State with the likes of Golda Meir, and David Ben-Gurion. David Ben-Gurion was born in my father's hometown of Plonsk, Poland in 1898. My dad said that David Ben-Gurion went to school with his grandmother Lazenski.

When the news came that Hitler crossed the border into Poland, thousands of Jewish young people started out on foot, aiming to go to Russia to escape the Nazis. The older people could not make the trip, but they sent their children on to "freedom." My dad, his sister

A Daughter of the Holocaust

and younger brother were also planning to make the trip to Russia on foot, leaving my grandparents behind. My dad shared that as they were leaving the house his mother cried and cried and cried. At that moment he describes his older sister slamming the door to the house shut. She said, "we're not going anywhere." They could not leave their parents alone to encounter the enemy. So as a family, minus the older brother Aaron, they stood together to face the Nazis. My dad and his siblings loved their parents too much to leave them knowing they probably would never see them again. Remembering his mother's tears was very difficult for my dad. He loved and respected his mother so much. The trauma of that day has always remained as vivid to him as if it had happened yesterday.

Before the transports started to the concentration camps, the Nazis placed all the Jews in my dad's town in a ghetto. There was much harassment and beatings and humiliation at the hands of the Nazis. My dad related a story about what happened on one of the High Holy Days, Rosh Hashanah, in his town. All the men were in the synagogue praying when the Nazis demanded that they leave the building and come into the courtyard. They proceeded to force every male to run back and forth and up and down the courtyard for hours, for no reason until they fell down from exhaustion. My father remembers watching his father do this knowing he was not a well man. It was heart wrenching for him.

My father and his family being Orthodox Jews attended synagogue in his town every Sabbath. He described the building as very large and very beautiful. When the Germans came to his town he remembers them coming to the synagogue taking the Torah Scroll out of the building into the courtyard. They proceeded to step on the scroll then tear it to pieces. My father, my grandfather and the other Orthodox men of the synagogue watched in horror as they desecrated and destroyed the Word of G-d. In the Jewish faith, if the Torah even touches the ground it is a desecration of G-d's name. They stood in shock and wondered how G-d could allow these Nazis to do this to His Word. They were crying out to G-d to cut off their hands and feet to stop them from doing what they were doing. Many of the men that witnessed this act turned away from G-d as a result. They were disheartened and lost faith.

The Germans entered Poland in 1939. Prior to this invasion, the Jews of the town of Plönsk lived, worked and intermingled with the Catholic Polish people of the town. Day by day, family-by-family, the Germans rounded up the Jews, took them from their homes and placed them in a Nazi-secured, closed off part of town (a ghetto). They had to leave their homes with little or none of their belongings. Two and three families were forced to live in one apartment. Very little food was allowed into the ghetto to feed the Jewish people forced to live there. They were required to wear a yellow patch, in the shape of a Jewish star, identifying them as Jews. The Nazis would frequently beat and harass and even kill many Jewish people at random. Under these conditions, the Jews were forced to do hard labor for the Germans. Many Jews died in the ghetto either by the gun or from starvation and disease due to the terrible living conditions forced upon them. In the ghetto they had the opportunity to bury their dead in the Jewish cemeteries. This occurred between the years 1939 and 1942.

In 1942, the Germans closed the ghetto in my father's town. All the remaining Jews, my father's family included, were taken to the train station. They were forced onto cattle cars and transported to the Auschwitz-Birkenau Concentration Camp. This concentration camp was on the border between Poland and Germany. Birkenau was on the Polish side and Auschwitz was on the German side. My dad was appalled that Poland allowed the Nazis to build the camp and the crematorium.

A picture capturing the horrors of a crematorium in a camp in Poland.
(Credit: Shutterstock)

AUSCHWITZ-BIRKENHAU

When my father arrived at Auschwitz with his family members and friends from his town, they realized how horrific their situation was. My father said he watched as many of his friends ran to the electrified wire gates that enclosed them and committed suicide. They knew they were not going to be able to take the conditions in the camps so they killed themselves. The thought crossed my dad's mind as well; however, he decided he was going to fight for his life. He said to himself, "Hitler is not going to kill me, I am going to survive". This he did by taking many risks and having much "mazel" (Yiddish for "blessing").

My father says he was liked by many of the German soldiers and he really didn't know why. He was given many indoor jobs to do so he did not have to work in the freezing cold with few clothes. He shared a story of he and his friend having to clean a German commander's office one day. While cleaning they found a large stack of cigarettes in the desk draw. They decided to take some of the cigarettes because they were a great bargaining chip to trade for food. When two officers came in to check on my dad and his friend, they noticed that cigarettes were missing (the stack was tilted). The two officers proceeded to beat them up very badly. Then one officer pointed his gun at my father's head ready to shoot him on the spot. The other officer pushed his hand away and said, "Leave him alone." My father's life was spared. That is "mazel".

My father frequently remembered and shared the story of a young woman named Shalamas. They went to school together. Her parents had a store next to his grandmother Lazenski's fruit store. When the Germans would go from store to store to find out who the Jews were, they would not believe that Shalamas was Jewish. My dad spoke of how very, very beautiful she was. She had blonde hair and blue eyes. She looked like she was part of the German "Aryan race". They did finally throw Shalamas into the cattle cars with my father and the rest of the Jews. My dad described how when she came out of the cattle car she was not the same. Shalamas did not survive long after that cattle car ride. My dad constantly remembered how beautiful Shalamas was and how the Nazis destroyed such beauty.

A Daughter of the Holocaust

When they got off the cattle cars after the transport, my father told of how two lines were formed. One line was for life and labor and the other line was for death and extermination. At this point, he and his brother and sister were separated from their parents. Both his parents, who were 40 years old, were too old to work so they were sent to their death. My dad could not describe the devastating effect that experience had on him and his siblings. He shared an account of a 36-year-old man who was pleading with the German soldiers to let him join the line for labor. This man could not understand why he was in the line for death. He felt he was strong enough to work. All his pleading was to no avail. The German soldiers would not let him leave the line he was on and he went to his death. Then, my father added, those in the line for labor would work and later die from disease or lack of food. The eventual fate of every Jew was the same in the eyes of the Nazis.

My eldest son Jason W. wrote this following poem for an assignment he had in the sixth grade.

"My People, My Blood"

My people were murdered
By a man who had no heart
For my people, my blood
Thinking of himself and power
He wiped out a nation
And left my people with nothing but
A nightmare of torture and death
Their families killed before their eyes
But some still live with that memory
And wish they were like the members
Of my people, my blood.

I was totally amazed at how, at the age of 11 years old, and not knowing very much about the Holocaust, he sat at the dining room table and wrote this poem in literally less than ten minutes. Jason had succeeded in capturing the essence of how my dad felt about the Holocaust. A question that always haunted my dad was, "Why did I survive and the rest of my family didn't?" He had a deep sense of guilt that he had lived and his family members died horrible deaths. Many survivors of the Holocaust share this same sense of guilt.

CHAI! LIFE!

In spite of my dad's feelings, he did survive the Holocaust. When he entered Auschwitz my dad, along with all the other Jews in the camp, stood in a long line to get a number tattooed on his arm. They all considered the number "the death number" thinking the end was near once given the tattoo. He was no longer referred to by his birth name but by the number on his arm. It was just another way for the Nazis to dehumanize the Jews. The number on my dad's arm was 84420. If you add up these numbers the total is eighteen. In the Jewish faith, the number "18" stands for the Hebrew word "Chai" which means "life" in English. My mother always told my dad that he survived the concentration camp because he was given that number on his arm.

At the end of the war, when the Germans knew they were defeated, many of the soldiers dropped their weapons and ran away so as not to be captured by the allied forces. Many of the Jews in the camp took up the guns and started killing any German soldiers they could. My dad said he was too weak to do that. Many of the Jews also raided nearby homes outside the gates of the camp and stole food and jewelry from the people in the homes. My dad did not do this either. He said stealing from the Germans would not bring his parents and siblings back from the dead. He did not want anything that belonged to the Germans.

As the war was coming to an end, the Nazis took my dad and the other prisoners from Auschwitz-Birkenau in Poland to Mauthausen Concentration Camp in Austria by train. They were finally liberated from Mauthausen in 1945. In Austria, the liberated prisoners were given food and a place to sleep. The Austrians took the guns away from the prisoners who were killing the Germans. They said, "There was enough killing." From Austria, those liberated were taken to Munich where the Red Cross was going to help them find any surviving family members.

AFTER LIBERATION

After a few days in Munich, American General Dwight David Eisenhower arrived to see first-hand what had happened. My dad saw Eisenhower and listened to him as he spoke to all the liberated prisoners. Eisenhower told them that the horror was now over - it was time to build a new life and to look to the future.

My husband and I went to visit the Holocaust Museum in Washington D.C. years later. Engraved on one of the walls as you enter the museum is a quote by General Dwight D. Eisenhower. It is as follows:

"The things I saw begs description... The visual evidence and the verbal testimony of starvation, cruelty and bestiality were so over-powering... I made the visit deliberately, in order to be in a position to give first-hand evidence of these things if ever, in the future, there develops a tendency to charge these allegations to propaganda."

Thank G-d for Eisenhower's insight and interest in the plight of the Jews after the war and that he had the wisdom and foresight to be a source of living "outside" proof that the Holocaust really did happen. My personal testimony is a source of living "inside" proof that the Holocaust really did happen. It is the account of my father's horrific experience in the Holocaust and the lasting effect on him and his offspring.

THE HOLOCAUST MUSEUM, WASHINGTON D.C.

When visiting the Holocaust Museum in Washington D.C. I noticed a feature that moved my heart immensely. In most museums the artifacts are roped off to prevent visitors from damaging or removing them from the premises. However, in this museum there were three different exhibits that you were permitted to get close to and touch. The first exhibit was an original cattle car taken from Auschwitz that transported the Jews to the various concentration camps. I was able to stand in such a train car and imagine my grandparents, my aunt, my uncle and my dad, in addition to scores of other Jews, forced to cram into a single car. They had no food or water for days. They were forced to stand for the entire trip. And there were no lavatory facilities for these people to use. I pictured my family suffering in this cattle car.

The second exhibit was an original bunk bed taken from Auschwitz that the prisoners were forced to sleep on. They were large shelves with slabs of wood on which to place your body. My father had described how 6 or 7 men had to squeeze into each shelf, which could only hold 3 or 4 men. I was able to stand in the museum, touching the bunk bed, again trying to experience what my family had to deal with. I must say it is beyond comprehension, but it still gave vivid imagery to what they had to endure.

In the third exhibit were concrete posts that surrounded the concentration camp upon which the barbed wire and electrical gates were mounted. These were the gates that my dad told me he watched his dear friends run to and grab hold of. They could not take the conditions in the camps so they killed themselves by electrocution. I stood touching these posts imaging those that committed suicide and being grateful that my father had not succumbed to such despair.

Another exhibit was an encasement full of old leather shoes that were worn by the prisoners in the camps. Above the case was a statement that read, "These leather shoes, the Nazis saw fit not to burn but the people who wore them they did." This is another sad example of man's inhumanity to man.

I feel my father's stories have become more three-dimensional as a result of seeing these exhibits in the museum. One major aspect, however, that is left out of every exhibit, every movie, and every documentary on the Holocaust are the smells that accompanied this horrific experience. A result of the unsanitary conditions, sickness and disease and the smell of dead and decaying bodies before and after the crematoriums. Adding this dimension would truly depict how incomprehensible the experience was for my father and all the other Jews at the hands of the Nazis.

SALVATION AND HEALING

I have been broken-hearted and sad for most of my life due to the events that occurred in my father's life and family. Many Jews blamed G-d for allowing the tragedy of the Holocaust to happen. Many ask where was G-d? Why did G-d not stop Hitler knowing that G-d can do anything? My father has asked these questions for years and years. I have asked these same questions myself. By the grace and mercy of G-d, I became a believer in Yeshua (Jesus) as the Promised Messiah of Israel in June of 1980. Studying the Scriptures and the life of Yeshua have resulted in a healing process that continues to this day.

Over the years I have come to know the character of G-d and the love of G-d. Yeshua, the Messiah, G-d's love manifest in human flesh, came to this earth to be the atonement for our sins. He experienced all that we experience as humans, our emotions, our physical needs, and our temptations all without sin. I have come to the realization that Yeshua, as a Jew, ("The King of the Jews"), experienced everything the Jews did in the Holocaust and much more during his time on earth at the hands of the Romans. And He too was innocent of any crime. Yeshua passed through worse treatment than the Nazis did to the Jews in the concentration camps if that can be fathomed.

So my G-d, who is complete love, can identify with the horrors my father and six million other Jews went through in the Holocaust. The details of Yeshua's experience can be found in the book of Isaiah, chapter 53 and Psalm 22 of the Bible. Yeshua came to atone for our transgressions with His own blood required by the Torah in the book of Leviticus chapter 17, verse 11. But more than that, Isaiah chapter 61 tells us the other reason why Yeshua came. He came to bring healing from all the effects of sin in this world as it says:

> "The Spirit of Adonai Elohim is upon me,
>   Because Adonai has anointed me
>   To announce good news to the poor.
>   He has sent me to heal the brokenhearted:
>   To proclaim freedom to the captives,
>   To let out into light those bound in the dark…
>   To comfort all who mourn, yes,
>   Provide for those in Tziyon who mourn,
>   Giving them garlands instead of ashes,
>   The oil of gladness instead of mourning,
>   A cloak of praise instead of a heavy spirit…"
>   (Isaiah 61:1-3)

I tried on many occasions to explain to my father that G-d did not cause the Holocaust. Man has free will to choose to sin or not to sin. Hitler and the many who followed him chose to do evil, to hate, to murder, to kill. It was not G-d because G-d is Love and the scripture above tells us about G-d's character and what He came to earth to do.

A dear friend wrote a song that touched my heart deeply in my healing process. It truly describes the heart of Yeshua, how He suffered (Isa. 53, Ps.22) and His love for those that suffered in the Holocaust or anyone who has suffered in this life for that matter (Isa. 61).

A Daughter of the Holocaust

" MY G-D"

My G-d, my G-d, why have you forsaken me
My G-d, my G-d, save me
My G-d, I cry out by day and night
I'm poured out like water, my bones are all out

Chorus:
Messiah came for you and me
To set the captives, the captives free
Surely goodness and love will follow me
And I will dwell in the house of the Lord

A band of evil men have circled me
They pierced my hands, and they pierced my feet
I count my bones and people stare
Does anyone, does anyone really care?

Chorus:

You, Oh Lord are my strength
You have rescued me from the lion's jaw
I will proclaim your name everyday
You will never hide your face from me

My father, all the other survivors, and even myself, consider
ourselves captives of the Holocaust. Yeshua, as the Bible says and
as the song says, came to set the captives free. In the book of Ezekiel
in the Bible, it talks about dry bones in the land of Israel coming to
life again. Another song written by my friend speaks of these dry
bones coming to life again. These are pictures of the millions of Jews
in these concentration camps that are dried up skeletons piled one

A Daughter of the Holocaust

on top of the other. The song says "Can these bones live?" Yes they can and they have through my Dad and the many survivors who migrated to Israel, the United States and many other countries of the world.

Having no known family when they were liberated, my Dad and about twenty fellow survivors stuck together not knowing what to do or where to go. In Europe, all survivors were allowed to travel the trains for free and in each country the Jewish organizations provided room and board for them. My dad and his friends were liberated in Austria then taken to Munich. They waited in Munich hoping to hear from some family member anywhere in the world.

Since they heard no news, my dad and his group began to travel around Europe. They went to Switzerland. They then crossed the Swiss (Austrian) Alps by foot to go to Italy. While on the Alps they got lost. If it were not for a man who lived on the Alps that spotted my dad and his friends, they would not have found their way out. They could have frozen to death in the dark of night in the Alps. G-d was still watching over my father on his journey even after the liberation.

My dad spent about a year in Italy with his friends. They took odd jobs to survive and he stayed with one Italian family. He told me he almost married a very beautiful Italian woman. However, she was not Jewish and his loyalty to his parents would not allow him to marry outside his religion. While in Italy, he shared a story about being given a meal made with rabbit. He really liked the meal. He said it tasted like chicken. When he was told that it was rabbit he got so sick to his stomach he threw up. He was not used to eating non-kosher food.

Murray, center, on top, below to the right, with friends in Munich

My father and his buddies were like family to each other. So after almost a year, they decided to go back to the Red Cross in Munich to see if any family members were still trying to contact any survivors. And one day, in this big room where they all waited day after day, my Dad's name was called. An aunt that lived in Boston was looking for any survivors from her family who lived in Plonsk, Poland. She was my Dad's mother's older sister. My dad then came to the United States by boat into a port in Boston. This is where he obtained the only remaining pictures of his mother, sister and grandmother. The Nazis destroyed any other physical memory of his family.

Picture: Murray, after arriving in America

The living arrangements with his aunt in Boston were not convenient so he was sent to his uncle in New York City. This uncle was his father's brother. And so my father settled in Brooklyn, living with his uncle and family. In Brooklyn my father became an apprentice to a barber. He then got his barber's license. He was able to partner with another Holocaust survivor and open his own business. It was in Brooklyn that he met and married my mother, a Jewish American-born woman nine years younger than himself. Her name was Jean Hauptman. She was the last of eight children. Her father was from Austria and her mother was from Hungry. They had immigrated to the United States at the turn of the century.

(Above) Eldest brother, Aaron Melach

(Right-Top) Visiting Aaron in Israel

(Right-Bottom) Mother, Niche Lazenski
Sol and older sister, Miriam

A Daughter of the Holocaust

Sadly, my mother died at the age of 38. My Dad was left to raise three children (my brother, Neil, 17 years old, my sister, Linda, 14 years old, and myself, Melanie, 13 years old) by himself. This past January, my mother will have been gone 51 years. My father never wanted to remarry because he did not want to bring a stepmother into the house. He stayed single for all those years for the sake of his children. He was a very faithful and dedicated father for which I am very grateful.

As I said earlier, I accepted Yeshua as my Messiah in 1980. I prayed for my dad for 25 years to accept Yeshua as his Messiah as well. Praise the Lord, in 2005, my father accepted Yeshua during a Rosh Hashanah Service at my congregation. A woman, whose father was also a Holocaust survivor, shared the Good News of Yeshua with him. She showed him that it was an evil man named Hitler who had innocent babies murdered and not G-d. In the summer of 2009, my dad went through the waters of immersion. I gratefully praise HaShem for answered prayer.

"Nothing Is Impossible With G-d!"

A Daughter of the Holocaust

In closing, both my father, and my siblings and I accepted Yeshua as our Atonement for our sins so when we die, we will go to be with G-d for eternity in Heaven.

If interested, the Scriptures (the Tanakh) prove Yeshua (Jesus) is the Promised Messiah of Israel. Look at Isaiah 9:6, Isaiah 7:14, Isaiah 53, Psalm 2 and many, many others. Take time if you can to look up these verses in the Bible, the Jewish Bible (the Tanakh). Pray to G-d to reveal to you if in fact Yeshua is the Messiah who came to die for our sins and is coming again to reign and rule the earth from Jerusalem. My family and I did this from only reading the Jewish Bible (the Tanakh) which allowed us to all believe and accept Yeshua.

We DID NOT convert to Christianity. We are still very Jewish and more so.

Here is a prayer you can pray to accept Yeshua into your heart as your Messiah and to repent of all your sins.

Yeshua, I repent of my sins and surrender my life to G-d. Wash me clean from my sins through the previous Blood of Yeshua that was shed for my sins and the sins of the whole world. As it says in Isaiah 53, I believe that Yeshua is G-d manifest in the flesh, that he died on the tree for my sins and rose again. I confess Yeshua as my Messiah and Savior and Lord. Come into my life, Yeshua. I love You and thank You for my salvation. Amen

A Daughter of the Holocaust

Documentation of my father's imprisonment in Auschwitz and Mauthausen, his U.S. naturalization certificate and ketubah (marriage certificate)

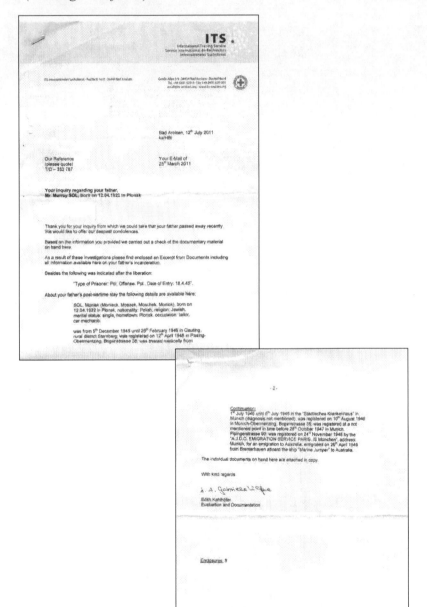

A Daughter of the Holocaust

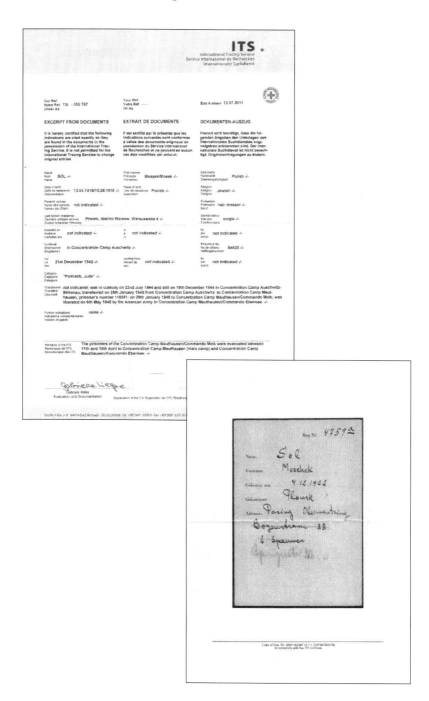

A Daughter of the Holocaust

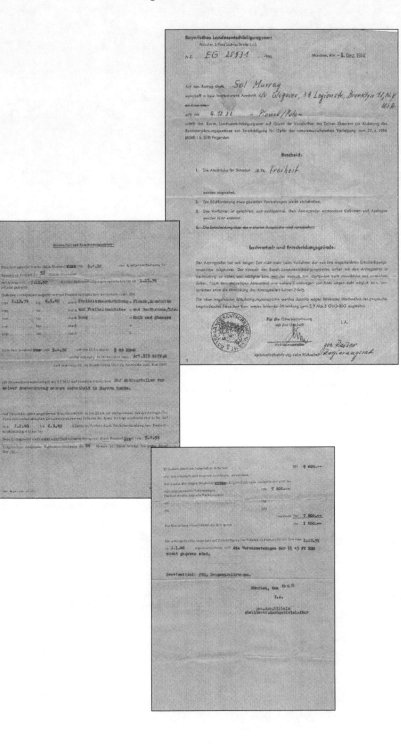

A Daughter of the Holocaust

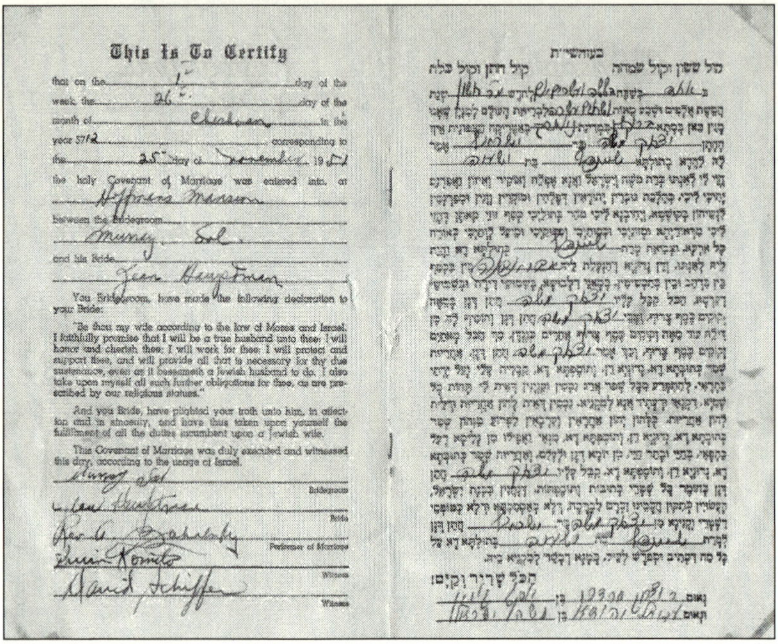

This Is To Certify

that on the 1st day of the week, the 26th day of the month of Cheshvan in the year 5712 corresponding to the 25th day of November 1951 the holy Covenant of Marriage was entered into, at Hoffmans Mansion between the Bridegroom Munz, Sol. and his Bride Jean Hegefman

You Bridegroom, have made the following declaration to your Bride:

"Be thou my wife according to the law of Moses and Israel. I faithfully promise that I will be a true husband unto thee: I will honor and cherish thee; I will work for thee; I will protect and support thee, and will provide all that is necessary for thy due sustenance, even as it beseemeth a Jewish husband to do. I also take upon myself all such further obligations for thee, as are prescribed by our religious statues."

And you Bride, have plighted your troth unto him, in affection and in sincerity, and have thus taken upon yourself the fulfillment of all the duties incumbent upon a Jewish wife.

This Covenant of Marriage was duly executed and witnessed this day, according to the usage of Israel.

Munz Sol — Bridegroom

[illegible] — Bride

[illegible] — Performer of Marriage

[illegible] Kowitz — Witness

David Schiffer — Witness

בעזהשי"ת

קול ששון וקול שמחה קול חתן וקול כלה

הכל שריר וקים

Manufactured by Amazon.ca
Bolton, ON